E. Brewster says: Be Encouraged!

31 Days of Encouragement

Volume 1: Building Your Faith

By

E. Brewster

E. Brewster says: *Be Encouraged!*

Copyright © 2018 by E. Brewster.

All rights reserved. This book or any portion thereof may not be reproduced or used in any manner whatsoever without the express written permission of the publisher
except for the use of brief quotations in a book review.

Printed in the United States of America.

First Printing, 2018

ISBN: 978-1984345141

E. Brewster says: *Be Encouraged!*

In loving memory of my sister.

Jamie Lynn Grant.
July 19, 1982 – December 29, 2017

E. Brewster says: *Be Encouraged!*

Day 1: Relax

Relax your mind. God has this under control... whatever "it" is...don't let "it" come between you and your Faith...

Breathe and Believe...

Word of the Day: Relax

Psalm 4:8 NIV
"In peace I will lie down and sleep, for you alone, Lord, make me dwell in safety."

E. Brewster says: *Be Encouraged!*

Day 2: Shine Bright

Let God's love shine through you today. Someone needs your smile, your hug, your apology, and your thank you...people are hurting bad... Take time to be selfless...

Show someone you care today.

Word of the Day: Shine

John 3:16 KJV
For God so loved the world, that he gave his only Son, that whoever believes in him should not perish but have eternal life.

E. Brewster says: *Be Encouraged!*

Day 3: Make It Happen

STOP waiting on people to support you... Get up and make it happen. You, Yourself, and God...

Word of the Day: You

Philippians 4:13 ESV
I can do all things through him who strengthens me.

E. Brewster says: *Be Encouraged!*

Day 4: You Survived

Broken but healed...in the storm but at Peace...alone but not Lonely...it looks doubtful but you remain Hopeful... you can't see it but you still believe it... you are a Survivor...more than a Conqueror...you are Winning...push through...

Word of the Day: Survivor

Jeremiah 31:2 KJV
Thus says the LORD, "The people who survived the sword found grace in the wilderness

E. Brewster says: *Be Encouraged!*

Day 5: Graced

Graced to see another amazing day...full of opportunity to spread love... We are here not by luck...but by Grace...make each moment count... Give thanks not just for but *in* everything...

Have a blessed day!!!

Word of the Day: Grace

Romans 5:1-2 NIV
Therefore, since we have been justified by faith, we have peace with God through our Lord Jesus Christ. Through him we have also obtained access by faith into this grace in which we stand, and we rejoice in hope of the glory of God.

E. Brewster says: *Be Encouraged!*

Day 6: Procrastination

Doubt is a form of fear that is often dressed up in procrastination... Don't be fooled...stay focused...

Let's Get it!

Word of the Day: Procrastination

Proverbs 13:4 ESV
The soul of the sluggard craves and gets nothing, while the soul of the diligent is richly supplied.

E. Brewster says: *Be Encouraged!*

Day 7: Clean Up

Unresolved issues from your past can disrupt your present... Things that you sweep under a rug will show up little by little each time that rug shifts...until you finally decide to clean what's hidden under the rug you will forever be plagued with old hurt... Deal with your issues before your issue deal with you...

Word of the Day: Resolve

Isaiah 43:18 NIV
"Forget the former things; do not dwell on the past."

E. Brewster says: *Be Encouraged!*

Reflections

You did it! You made it through the first seven days of encouragement. We often give up when the trial seems to go against our favor. Remember the fight is fixed. We win! Trust God.

Keep pushing.
Breathe and Believe.
Let's Go!

E. Brewster says: *Be Encouraged!*

Day 8: Don't Worry

His (God) love will see you through... Don't worry just Breathe, Believe, and prepare for your Breakthrough.

Word of the Day: Believe

Hebrews 13:6 ESV
So we can confidently say, "The Lord is my helper; I will not fear; what can man do to me?"

Day 9: Nothing To Lose

Believe me when I say that your faith works. Try it...Speak it...Declare it...Believe it...Do it...Get up and put your faith to work...You have nothing to lose and everything to gain... God is able!

Word of the Day: Faith

Matthew 21:22 NLT
"You can pray for anything, and if you have faith, you will receive it."

E. Brewster says: *Be Encouraged!*

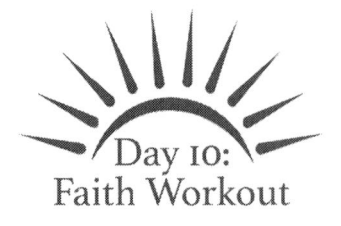

Day 10: Faith Workout

Your Faith may be experiencing a workout and it may not feel good right now... but remember God is making you stronger right now.

Word of the Day: Stronger

James 2:17 ESV
So also faith by itself, if it does not have works, is dead.

E. Brewster says: *Be Encouraged!*

Day 11: Rise Up

Be determined to rise above the ashes of your issues and grab hold to your Victory...Take your victory by force...it's yours...

Word of the Day: Rise

Psalms 20:5 NIV
May we shout for joy over your victory and lift up our banners in the name of our God. May the LORD grant all your requests.

E. Brewster says: *Be Encouraged!*

Day 12: Everything Will Be Alright

The "everything's going to be alright" feeling is Him (God) confirming His presence...

Word of the Day: God

Genesis 28:15 NIV
"I am with you and will watch over you wherever you go, and I will bring you back to this land. I will not leave you until I have done what I have promised you."

E. Brewster says: *Be Encouraged!*

Day 13: Transformation

Sometimes when you are in transition you can feel unsure, unsettled, unfocused, and uneasy...but don't let those feelings undo your progress. Keep moving forward. You are being transformed...

Word of the Day: Transformation

Romans 12:2 KJV
And be not conformed to this world: but be ye transformed by the renewing of your mind, that ye may prove what is that good, and acceptable, and perfect, will of God.

E. Brewster says: *Be Encouraged!*

Day 14: Live

Love hard, forgive quick, smile on purpose, live life while you are alive...

Word of the Day: Alive

John 15:12 KJV
This is my commandment, That ye love one another, as I have loved you.

E. Brewster says: *Be Encouraged!*

Reflections

Look at you! You are fourteen days in. Each day you are growing stronger and stronger. Don't let anyone or anything come between you and your journey. Keep pushing forward.

Let's Go!

E. Brewster says: *Be Encouraged!*

Day 15: No Doubt

When Hope consumes your heart...there is no room for doubt...

Word of the Day: Hope

Psalm 39:7 KJV
And now, Lord, what wait I for? my hope is in thee.

E. Brewster says: *Be Encouraged!*

Day 16: Faith Works

Faith is an action word...if you don't work it…you won't see results. Put your faith into action. It works!

Word of the Day: Work

James 2:22 NASB
You see that faith was working with his works, and as a result of the works, faith was perfected.

E. Brewster says: *Be Encouraged!*

Day 17: He Will Heal The Hurt

They say putting Neosporin on a wound not only helps it heal faster but it heals it so you can barely see the scar. Any wound you have right now... let Jesus be your Neosporin.

Word of the Day: Healing

Luke 1:37 For with God nothing shall be impossible.

E. Brewster says: *Be Encouraged!*

Day 18: Stability

When life gets Shaky...I'm thankful that God is my stabilizer...

Word of the Day: Stable

Psalms 16:5 NET
Lord, you give me stability and prosperity; you make my future secure.

E. Brewster says: *Be Encouraged!*

Day 19: Inner Strength

God has given each and every one of us the inner strength to achieve what we think is impossible. Set your hearts and minds on your goals and move forward with purpose. With God all things are possible! Sometimes it's hard...but you must Believe to Achieve!

Word of the Day: Strength

2 Cor 12:9 KJV
And he said unto me, My grace is sufficient for thee: for my strength is made perfect in weakness. Most gladly therefore will I rather glory in my infirmities, that the power of Christ may rest upon me.

E. Brewster says: *Be Encouraged!*

Day 20: Misery Loves Company

You don't have to keep Misery company...be around people who choose to smile on purpose...people who will dance in the rain...

Word of the Day: Smile

Prov 18:20 ISV
The positive words that a man speaks fill his stomach; he will be satisfied with what his lips produce.

E. Brewster says: *Be Encouraged!*

Day 21: Testify

God will use your troubled past as your present testimony...help somebody overcome their struggle by the strength within your testimony...

Word of the Day: Testimony

Psalm 68:11 KJV
The Lord gave the word: great was the company of those that published it.

E. Brewster says: *Be Encouraged!*

Reflections

Way to go! Twenty-one days in. You are building your Faith each day. Keep moving forward. Don't let the enemy creep in. Keep yourself surrounded by positivity.

You can do it!

Let's Go!

E. Brewster says: *Be Encouraged!*

Day 22: God's Ability

What you think can't happen through you...God is preparing you to do...Take your eyes off your own ability and walk in God's ability. He will equip you for your purpose...

Word of the Day: Purpose

Hebrews 13:20
ISV equip you with everything good to do his will, accomplishing in us what pleases him through Jesus, the Messiah. To him be glory forever and ever! Amen.

E. Brewster says: *Be Encouraged!*

Day 23: God's Plan

Your issues do not stop God's plan. Keep on pushing... Keep on believing... Yes, Faith takes work...but it works...

Word of the Day: Plan

2 Corinthians 9:8 KJV
And God is able to make all grace abound toward you; that ye, always having all sufficiency in all things, may abound to every good work.

E. Brewster says: *Be Encouraged!*

Day 24: Stop Worrying

STOP WORRYING! Your emotions tend to run all over the place when you're worried. Slow down...take a deep breath...take a minute...and calm yourself... tell your emotions they can take the day off... Better yet tell your emotions that God's got this... No need for worrying...

Word of the Day: Calm

Psalm 37:7 KJV
Rest in the LORD, and wait patiently for him.

E. Brewster says: *Be Encouraged!*

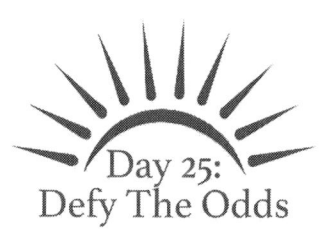

Day 25: Defy The Odds

Have Hope that defies statistics...and have Faith that sees Greater... God is able and He won't fail... I know Faith is work...but I also know it truly works...with action...

Word of the Day: Action

Psalm 37: 5 KJV
Commit thy way unto the LORD; trust also in him; and he shall bring it to pass.

E. Brewster says: *Be Encouraged!*

Day 26: Get Up

We are stronger because we faced it...we are wiser because each trial taught us a lesson...we are better because we are no longer phased by the tricks of the enemy...we are Survivors. We don't give up we Get Up! We know God is in control...

Keep on pushing...

Word of the Day: Push

John 16:33 KJV
These things I have spoken unto you, that in me ye might have peace. In the world ye shall have tribulation: but be of good cheer; I have overcome the world.

E. Brewster says: *Be Encouraged!*

Day 27: Encourage Yourself

I know what's coming is far better than what's been. "I will not be phased by what I see because I know God is working it out for me...I believe...I'm pushing into my purpose..."

Word of the Day: Encourage

Deuteronomy 31:6 NASB
"Be strong and courageous, do not be afraid or tremble at them, for the LORD your God is the one who goes with you He will not fail you or forsake you."

E. Brewster says: *Be Encouraged!*

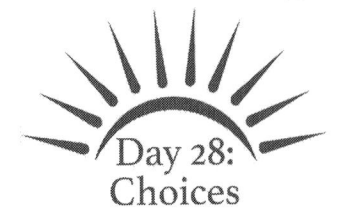

Day 28: Choices

You are in charge of how YOU feel today. Choose to be Joyful...choose to be Peaceful...choose to be Hopeful...choose Happiness...it's your choice...choose wisely.

Word of the Day: Choices

Psalm 119:30 NASB
I have chosen the faithful way; I have placed Your ordinances before me.

E. Brewster says: *Be Encouraged!*

Reflections

Twenty-eight days of hard work. Keep up the great work. Your strength is encouraging others. Push through! Let's Go!

E. Brewster says: *Be Encouraged!*

Day 29: My God Is Bigger

Please know that nothing you are facing at the moment is bigger than the God you serve...believe beyond the limits... God is able...

Word of the Day: Nothing

Exodus 15:6 KJV
Thy right hand, O LORD, is become glorious in power: thy right hand, O LORD, hath dashed in pieces the enemy.

E. Brewster says: *Be Encouraged!*

Day 30: Even In Chaos

When everything around you is in chaos...don't forget that even in chaos you can find Peace...even in despair there is Hope...when fear creeps in remember your Faith...and always give thanks...not just for everything but in everything... God is...all you need and more...

Word of the Day: Peace

Psalm 107:29 KJV
He maketh the storm a calm, so that the waves thereof are still.

E. Brewster says: *Be Encouraged!*

Day 31: Stay Focused

Little issues come to distract you from your BIG blessings! Stay FOCUSED. God is good...give thanks...not just for everything but in everything...

Word of the Day: Focused

1 John 3:3 KJV
And every man that hath this hope in him purifieth himself, even as he is pure.

E. Brewster says: *Be Encouraged!*

Reflections

You did it! Thirty-One days of being positive. You didn't let the tricks of the enemy fool you. You kept moving despite it all. Look at you now. You are a Conqueror. Be proud. You are Courageous. Keep it up. Encourage others. This world needs you right now. Let's Go and help others Grow!

Greater

Let the rain fall, our FAITH will weather the storm...let the earth shake, our HOPE will not be changed... let people say it will never happen, our FAITH will ignore the doubt... things may get dark and hard to see but our HOPE is the light that will get us through...our FAITH will endure through the worst conditions...our HOPE will stand when others expect us to fall...no matter what we see in front of us the Faith in us sees greater... ~E. Brewster says *Be Encouraged!*

E. Brewster says: *Be Encouraged!*

2 Samuel 22:3 KJV
The God of my rock; in him will I trust: he is my shield, and the horn of my salvation, my high tower, and my refuge, my saviour; thou savest me from violence.

Made in the USA
Coppell, TX
17 December 2021